LYNN CURLEE
SKYSCRAPER

Atheneum Books for Young Readers
NEW YORK   LONDON   TORONTO   SYDNEY   NEW DELHI

"Towers are for power." —Philip Johnson, architect

It is the crown jewel of the New York City skyline, a soaring tower, capped by a fantastic spire—a series of gleaming metal arches punctuated with an exuberant sunburst arrangement of sharply pointed triangular windows. The arches recede as they ascend, finally tapering to a slender central spike that seems to pierce the clouds like the tip of a gigantic needle. On beautiful days sunlight glances off the polished chrome-nickel steel high above the city streets so that the arches glitter and sparkle, as though studded with diamonds. The spire belongs to the Chrysler Building, a skyscraper named for its original owner, Walter P. Chrysler, the automobile tycoon; and if ever there was a building guaranteed to make you smile, this is the one. Besides its unique spire, the Chrysler Building sports patterned brickwork laid around metal hubcaps to suggest car wheels, and four gigantic, winged radiator caps adorn its lower bastions. Best of all, eight spectacular eagle-head gargoyles, like titanic hood ornaments, jut from corners high up on the flanks of the tower, guarding the upper floors and spire.

The Chrysler Building has another claim to fame besides its remarkable decoration. When completed in 1930, it was the tallest structure ever erected by man. It held this title for just eleven months, until the Empire State Building, an even bigger skyscraper under construction a few blocks away, topped off a couple of hundred feet higher. The Empire State and Chrysler Buildings are among the most famous buildings in the world, and for decades they were unchallenged in height.

Since the dawn of civilization, people have tried to reach for the sky by building tall structures. Only a century after the invention of stone architecture, the Egyptians built the Great Pyramid at Giza, a funeral monument 481 feet high—the tallest man-made object in the world for nearly 4,500 years. In the ancient Near East, ziggurats like artificial mountains provided platforms for temples and for astronomical observations. Towering gothic cathedrals aspired toward heaven in medieval Europe, and later, lofty baroque domes were built for popes and kings. In Central America the stepped pyramids of the Maya and Aztecs served as high altars for rituals, while in the Far East, Indian stupas, Chinese pagodas, and Japanese fortified castles all display the natural impulse of the human spirit to build tall structures. But just *how* tall has always depended upon technology.

ie Chrysler Building, with the Empire State Building
der construction in the background

For thousands of years, in advanced societies, the most important buildings were made of stone. The tallest stone structure ever built is the immense marble obelisk dedicated as a monument to our first president, George Washington, in Washington, D.C. Finished in 1885, the monument is 555 feet high and was the first structure in all of history taller than the Great Pyramid.

Only four years after the Washington Monument was completed, the height record was shattered. French engineer Gustave Eiffel built an enormous tower in Paris as the centerpiece of the International Exposition of 1889. A viewing platform commemorating the centennial of the French Revolution, the Eiffel Tower was also a stunning demonstration of a revolutionary new technology. It is constructed of iron girders bolted together to form a latticework frame. A metal frame structure is very strong, and it can go very high—much higher than stone. And at an audacious, breathtaking 986 feet, the Eiffel Tower is nearly twice the height of the Washington Monument. It was by far the world's tallest structure for exactly forty years—until the Chrysler Building topped it.

The skyscraper is a uniquely American invention. From early innovations in the late 1800s, the tall multistory building came of age in Chicago and New York. The first ones were simply office buildings. Today skyscrapers are built in cities around the world, and besides offices, they now often house hotels, restaurants, theaters, concert halls, residences, shopping malls, and even parks. One hundred years ago, a 10-story building was considered a skyscraper, but now there are several buildings that top 100 stories, and immense buildings approaching 200 stories have even been seriously proposed. They are more than just buildings; they are marvels of modern technology and spectacular emblems of power and wealth. The skyscraper has become the iconic symbol of urban life in our modern world. It has been called the "shaper of cities and fortunes."

"It must be every inch a proud and soaring thing."

—Louis Sullivan, architect

During the late nineteenth century, American society was changing radically. After the Civil War, a vibrant new urban society arose in the rapidly growing big cities, fueled by immigration and industry and financed by commercial enterprise. Over time a new kind of building gradually evolved to meet society's business needs—a place where large numbers of people go to work at desks every day—the office building. Offices are built by businessmen whose aim is making a profit, so as cities grew more dense, and land became more valuable, the natural impulse was to build taller buildings to provide more rentable space.

No one simply sat at a drawing board and designed the first skyscraper. Instead, a brand-new way of constructing a building was developed over several decades, thanks to a series of amazing technological advances that made it possible to build higher than ever before. The key to building skyscrapers was metal frame construction. In the 1850s an efficient process for manufacturing steel was invented. Architects and engineers now had a revolutionary new material to work with. Steel is rigid and strong, but relatively light and inexpensive. A tall stone building must have extremely thick walls to support the immense weight. The taller the structure, the thicker (and more expensive) the walls must be. Now, instead of expensive walls of stone, a simple yet extremely strong grid of steel girders could be erected quickly to bear the entire weight of an office building, exactly like the skeleton supporting your body. The exterior walls now could be merely a skin of any suitable weatherproof material covering the framework, and need not bear any weight. This ingenious idea is called curtain wall construction.

The safety elevator was another critical innovation that encouraged tall buildings. The first passenger elevator was installed in a New York department store in 1857, and the technology spread rapidly. Now for the first time it was possible for people to have easy access to the upper floors of much taller buildings. In addition, electric power, first available in the early 1880s, was crucial for adequate lighting, and efficient plumbing and heating were vital for comfort. Finally, the telephone, the typewriter, and the mimeograph, a kind of primitive copy machine, were also

THE DEVELOPMENT OF SKYSCRAPER TECHNOLOGY

STEEL FRAME CONSTRUCTION

The first metal used in construction was cast iron. By the mid-nineteenth century, engineers were building immense bridges, rail stations, and exhibition halls with iron frames. In 1856 Sir Henry Bessemer patented a process for manufacturing steel, which is much stronger and harder than iron. By the 1880s steel was being mass-produced cheaply.

THE PASSENGER ELEVATOR

Elevators began as simple hoists for freight. In 1853 Elisha Otis invented a safety mechanism to prevent an elevator from falling. The first commercial passenger elevator was installed in a New York department store in 1857. At first, elevators were steam-powered. They were electrified beginning in 1889.

ELECTRICITY

Thomas Edison invented the electric light in 1879. He also built the first electrical power station and distribution system in New York in 1881. From this beginning, the technology of electric power spread rapidly to all parts of the country.

PLUMBING AND HEATING

By the mid-nineteenth century, the big cities were building waterworks and sewage systems. During the same era, the flush toilet was developed and gradually improved, and by the 1880s, it was in wide use. For heat, most large buildings had steam boilers, with pipes carrying the steam to radiators throughout the building.

COMMUNICATIONS

The first practical typewriter was developed in 1868. By the 1880s it was being mass-produced. The mimeograph machine was invented in 1876. In the same year, Alexander Graham Bell invented the telephone, and by the mid-1880s telephone service was expanding rapidly.

developed during this period, providing the office worker with essential tools. By the mid-1880s all of these innovations were in use in Chicago.

The Windy City was a boomtown—a burgeoning city on the edge of the prairie frontier, connected by rail and water with the urban east. Chicago was brash and raw, attracting bold men with new ideas. A disastrous fire had destroyed the main business district in 1871, and in a frenzy of building, the city remade itself. In this atmosphere, all of the new technology came together in the Home Insurance Building, built in 1884 by architect William LeBaron Jenney. It was a 10-story office building with a steel frame, and it is generally considered to be the first complete example of this new type of building.

Unlike older and simpler kinds of structures, the tall office building is a complex arrangement of different systems. The metal frame is the structural system. The elevators form a transportation system. The mechanical system includes the electrical wiring as well as heating and plumbing lines. The complicated construction process must be planned and coordinated so that these interlocked systems come together properly. First the site is excavated. Steel and concrete columns called piles are laid as a foundation to transfer the weight of the finished structure to the rock or soil underneath. Then steel girders are lifted by cranes and hoists and bolted together in a grid to make the metal frame. As the framework rises story by story, a concrete floor is laid between each one. Workers on lower stories can begin "hanging" the exterior curtain wall. Once the building is enclosed, the transportation and mechanical systems are installed, embedded within the structure. The interior spaces of the building are finished last.

Although it was innovative, the Home Insurance Building looked just like the masonry office buildings that surrounded it. Faced in a thin layer of stone and brick, it seemed massive and heavy with horizontal rows of windows. There was no way to tell that the structure was actually a steel frame. Jenney's innovations were technical, not artistic, and they were immediately taken up by a new generation of Chicago architects. These men invented a unique style for tall buildings with a series of practical and utilitarian flat-topped office structures in the late 1880s and 1890s. Ranging in height between 10 and 20 stories, their buildings were the first to be called "skyscrapers," a term borrowed from nautical slang referring to the high masts of tall ships.

The Home Insurance Building under construction

One of these architects was a real artist. His name was Louis Sullivan and most of his major work was done in Chicago, but the building that many consider his masterpiece was built in Buffalo, New York, in 1895. The Guaranty Building has 13 stories—a lofty cubic tower raised on a base of storefronts, with a gigantic overhanging cornice at the top. The grid of the steel frame is hinted at by the terra-cotta panels of the curtain wall that covers it. But the design is subtle and refined, with an emphasis on vertical lines, so that the eye is constantly led upward. It is practical as well as handsome, and it looks like nothing but an office building.

In a time when most architects turned to the past for inspiration, Sullivan realized that skyscrapers were something brand-new and fundamentally different than any other kind of building. *Form follows function* was his famous motto. By this he meant that the purpose and structure of a building should somehow be expressed in the way it looks. Of the skyscraper he wrote: "It is lofty. It must be tall. Every inch of it tall. The force and power of altitude must be in it, the glory and pride of exaltation must be in it. It must be every inch a proud and soaring thing." Louis Sullivan's philosophical ideas were even more important than his buildings and were very influential on the future of architecture.

"A machine that makes the land pay." —Cass Gilbert, architect

Despite Chicago's lead in skyscraper design, at the beginning of the twentieth century the real action shifted to New York, by far the biggest city in America, and the undisputed center of finance, trade, and culture. Already densely crowded with buildings, the Big Apple had nowhere to go but up.

However, instead of form following function, in New York, form followed the fashion of building in historical styles. The first great New York skyscraper is the Flatiron Building. It was built in 1902 on a triangular sliver of land between Fifth Avenue and Broadway. Thanks to the eccentric site, the 22-story building forms a dramatic narrow wedge, like a vertical blade or the prow of a ship steaming up the avenue. It looked so unusual that at first people were afraid the wind would blow it over! Here, instead of revealing the steel frame in the Chicago manner, the entire structure is covered with terra-cotta panels molded to resemble the stonework of a

French Renaissance château. Since it didn't fall down, the Flatiron was an instant sensation, and at once became a symbol of the city.

In New York, architects first began really striving for great height. Buildings were being built taller and taller, and architects *did* have to begin designing their structures to withstand the force of wind as well as gravity. In 1908 the Singer Building topped off at 47 stories—over 600 feet. The first skyscraper taller than the Washington Monument, it was also the first soaring tower on the city's rapidly changing skyline. Ungainly and awkward, the Singer Building was not beautiful, but it certainly was tall. At 50 stories, the 700-foot Metropolitan Life Insurance Company Tower of 1909 was both taller *and* quite beautiful. It was designed as a gigantic superscale replica of an actual historical building—the famous Campanile, or bell tower, in St. Mark's Square, Venice. This association gave it a kind of instant "class," with the ideas of solidity and tradition attached. Utterly distinctive and visible from all over town, Met Life Tower quickly became the symbol of the company that built it. It was becoming evident that a skyscraper could be more than just a building.

Frank W. Woolworth was a retailing genius who had made a fortune from his five-and-dime stores, and he wanted a prestigious symbol for his own company. In 1913 architect Cass Gilbert gave him the tallest skyscraper yet. The Woolworth Building is a great block 29 stories tall, with a beautiful soaring tower that reaches to 57 stories, or just under 800 feet. It was Gilbert's inspiration to design his building in the Gothic style of medieval cathedrals. The entire structure is clad in white terra-cotta panels resembling gothic stonework. Vertical piers carry the eye upward in an unbroken line from the sidewalk to a spire that is crowned by a green copper pinnacle surrounded by buttresses and gargoyles. This impressive building was even known as the "Cathedral of Commerce." It has a stately dignity that elevates it to the status of a monument dedicated to the idea that business can be regarded as a noble endeavor—a civic enterprise that benefits society. The Woolworth Building is the great masterpiece of the early New York "historical" skyscrapers, and one of the major landmarks of the skyline.

Woolworth's architect Cass Gilbert remarked that a skyscraper is "a machine that makes the land pay." And by making buildings ever bigger and taller, with greater floor area for rent, the land could be made to pay more and more. The Woolworth, Met Life Tower, Singer, and Flatiron buildings were only the most celebrated of the

early New York skyscrapers. All over lower Manhattan, property owners and developers were gradually tearing down the old city and erecting tall buildings—seeking profits of their own. But lower Manhattan was rapidly becoming incredibly congested, its narrow, crooked streets like dismal canyons between great looming cliffs. Many people, including architects, began to question the desirability of building skyscrapers. These huge buildings were radically changing the nature of the city. As one critic wrote, "the excessively tall building constitutes a menace to public health and safety . . . shutting out the light of the heavens and circumscribing the air of the streets." Would the metropolis of the future be grand or grim?

A critical limit was reached with the Equitable Building of 1915. It was "only" 41 stories tall, but it was a vast cubic structure that took up an entire city block—the most massive skyscraper yet built and the biggest office building in the world. It was also totally undistinguished, criticized as resembling an immense filing cabinet, and seen as "nothing more than a device to cram more floors into the sky." The Equitable cast a broad shadow for blocks around, and it galvanized public opinion. Partly as a result, New York was the first city to pass zoning laws restricting developers and builders from doing whatever they wanted. From now on, architects were required to build up in steps, providing setbacks for upper floors and towers, allowing light to reach the streets below.

With the coming of World War I in the mid-teens, skyscraper construction was halted for a few years. Steel was needed for armaments, and there was a labor shortage. And when the war ended late in 1918, America had become a different place. The horse and carriage of the Gilded Age had finally and totally given way to the automobile, streetcar, and subway of a more mechanized world. Airplanes and airships, which had been used as weapons of war, now promised a new ease of travel. As the decade of the 1920s began, radio and movies suddenly became powerful mediums of mass entertainment. Like the skyscraper, all of these technologies were first developed in the years around the turn of the century, and they all came to maturity after the war in the Roaring Twenties, a time of peace, prosperity, and profound cultural change in America.

The first important architectural event of the new decade was a 1922 competition to design "the most beautiful and distinctive office building in the world" for the

Chicago Tribune newspaper. More than two hundred architects from twenty-three different countries entered the contest. A handsome gothic tower crowned with a ring of heavy buttresses by Raymond Hood and John Meade Howells won the $50,000 prize, and today it is one of Chicago's great skyscrapers. But some of the entries from Europe were even more interesting. One design looked almost like a machine, with a bare steel frame filled in with curtain walls of glass. The most startling plan was a tower in the form of a single titanic Greek column. Second prize was given to Finnish architect, Eliel Saarinen. His skyscraper design had a massive slab of a tower with blocky setbacks, strong vertical lines, and no historical style. It resembled a sculpted mountain, and it almost won.

With its innovative setbacks, Saarinens's design demonstrated a beautiful way to conform to the strict New York zoning law, and it became the model for a new style of skyscraper. Raymond Hood adopted this new style in his design for the American Radiator Building of 1924. It is a modest tower of only 22 stories, but it is very dramatic. Clad in black brick, so that the windows almost disappear, it seems to be molded out of solid rock. The setbacks near the top have carved and gilded decoration, so that from a distance the elegant tower resembles the summit of a dark craggy peak dusted with gold.

American Radiator was among the first of an incredible series of great skyscrapers that were built in New York during the 1920s. From lower Manhattan to midtown, architects tried to outdo one another. Practical Chicago-style structures were erected next to dignified classical towers. An Aztec-style temple might crown one spire, right across the street from a lofty Renaissance palazzo. But the best of the new skyscrapers were distinctive and unique—nonhistorical and streamlined, sweeping up from the sidewalk like cliffs and rising in steps, with bold blocky "masses slicing into the air." Dramatic and theatrical, they were lavishly decorated, often with carved trim or brilliantly colored terra-cotta panels in an energetic new style called "art deco" that perfectly captures the exuberant spirit of the age. It was a golden era of skyscraper construction when people could imagine a futuristic "Metropolis of Tomorrow"—a gleaming city of broad avenues lined with dazzling towers connected by soaring bridges and elevated highways; the sky full of taxi-planes and personal dirigibles.

"How high can you make it so that it won't fall down?"

—John J. Raskob, real estate investor

For sixteen years the venerable Woolworth Building was the peak of the New York City skyline, and the tallest skyscraper in the world. But at the end of the 1920s, it lost its title. Two new soaring towers were under construction at the same time, and both had passed the 900-foot mark. Downtown at 40 Wall Street, architect Craig Severance was completing a 66-story tower topped by a lofty pyramid crown for the Manhattan Company, while in midtown Walter Chrysler's skyscraper was inching upward. No one was quite sure which would be taller. William Van Alen, Chrysler's architect, and Severance had once been business partners. Now they were competing in a race for the sky.

Van Alen had changed the design of his spire several times, but once the steel frame for the dramatic crowning arches was in place, it was announced that the Chrysler Building would have 77 stories, at 925 feet. When the pyramid crown atop 40 Wall Street was finished off at 927 feet, it was declared the new champion by two feet. But Van Alen was not finished. One day late in 1929, he watched from the sidewalk several blocks away as his plan unfolded. From deep within the building, a needle-sharp spike slowly emerged from the summit, "like a butterfly from a cocoon," and slowly climbed to a height of 1,046 feet. It had been assembled secretly in an airshaft and in ninety minutes it was hoisted into place. With this theatrical gesture, the Chrysler Building was now the tallest structure ever built.

Walter Chrysler spared no expense in making it the most flamboyant of all skyscrapers and a unique advertisement for his company. The lobby is lined in opulent red marble, while the exquisite elevator cabs are paneled with elaborate art deco patterns of metal and wood inlay. At the very summit, there was originally a small observatory room, decorated with painted sun rays, starbursts, and art deco saturn lights.

The Chrysler Building's spike was raised on October 23, 1929. With supremely ironic timing, on the very next day the stock market began to crash, and the nation gradually and relentlessly slid into an era of severe economic hardship that would last an entire decade. The Roaring Twenties were over. It was the beginning of the Great Depression of the 1930s.

Inside the Chrysler Building Observatol

But the race for the sky was not quite done. While the Chrysler Building was being finished, ground was broken a few blocks away on Fifth Avenue for a far more massive structure. As the economy and the mood of the nation plunged, the greatest skyscraper of all was rising into the sky. The Empire State Building was erected from foundation to spire in an astonishing thirteen months to open in May 1931. Architect William Lamb thoroughly planned the construction process to an unusual degree in advance, almost like a military campaign. When construction was going at full speed, a new floor of steel framing was added every day by dauntless steelworkers who risked their lives balancing on narrow beams high above the city streets. As many as 3,400 people were working on the Empire State Building at the same time. A number of these men were Native Americans, who had a reputation for working fearlessly at great heights. They were grateful to have good jobs during the dark days of the early depression.

The building they made is superlative in every way. Its construction statistics are astounding. The Empire State Building contains about 60,000 tons of structural steel, 62,000 cubic yards of concrete, 10 million bricks, 200,000 square feet of limestone, and 730 tons of aluminum and stainless steel on the exterior. There are 75 miles of water pipes and 2 million feet of electrical wires, as well as 73 elevators and 6,500 windows. It would take a train 57 miles long to haul all of the materials used in its construction. The handsome tower at first topped off at 86 floors, then a dramatic metal spire was added to bring it to 102 stories for a height of 1,250 feet. The entire structure is clad in a curtain wall of dignified gray limestone, with vertical chrome-nickel stripes and just a hint of art deco ornament. It is streamlined and stately, and very grand.

The entrance lobby is a lavish display of art deco design with richly veined marble and sleek metal trim, and the summit has a large outdoor deck that goes around all four sides for a thrilling bird's-eye view of the entire bustling metropolis far below. Originally the crowning spire above the observation deck was planned to serve as a mooring mast for airships. But this feat was tried only once in 1931. When a small dirigible attempted to dock, even a slight updraft caused the pilot nearly to lose control, and the dubious idea of an airship port was quickly abandoned as unsafe. Because of this relentless updraft, snow appears to fall upward at the top of the skyscraper!

The Empire State Building instantly took its place as the ultimate icon of New York City. Its dramatic profile dominates the midtown skyline, and its observation deck is a top tourist attraction. In 1933 it was even one of the stars of a hit movie. The startling image of the gargantuan gorilla King Kong, scaling the great skyscraper while being buzzed by tiny biplanes, is one of the most famous in all of American popular culture.

The Empire State Building's structural solidity was proved in 1945, when a plane, lost in dense fog, crashed into the 79th floor. Fortunately, it was a Saturday and the building was nearly empty. Still, 14 people were killed. Amazingly, the structure remained sound, and the damage was quickly repaired. The Empire State Building would be the world's tallest building for over 40 years, and it came to be regarded with awe and affection, acquiring almost the mythic status of a natural wonder like Niagara Falls or Grand Canyon.

In the depths of the Great Depression only a few skyscraper projects that were already underway before the crash were completed. A golden age of skyscraper construction slowly came to an end. The Depression was followed by the disastrous cataclysm of World War II. For more than a decade there were very few new skyscrapers. But by now New York had taken its place as the world's greatest metropolis. At midcentury, Manhattan looked like no other place on earth. Walt Whitman, the great American poet, once called New York a "city of spires and masts." He was referring to the tall ships and church steeples of the nineteenth-century city, but now the spires and masts of great skyscrapers gave Whitman's phrase a new resonance. The very emblem of New York City was a jagged skyline bristling with glittering skyscrapers, a fabulous display of American wealth, power, progress, sophistication, and glamour.

"Architecture is the real battleground of the spirit."

—Ludwig Mies van der Rohe, architect

During the first third of the twentieth century, skyscraper technology spread to every big city in America. Besides Chicago, with its rich tradition of tall buildings, cities such as Philadelphia, St. Louis, and Detroit began to develop skylines. And by the '30s even many small cities throughout the country had one or two modest skyscrapers. But so far, the only skyscrapers were in America.

Despite the upheaval of two world wars, Louis Sullivan's important ideas about form and function were taken up by a generation of European architects. Although they built no skyscrapers there, they did take his ideas to the limit by developing a revolutionary new style for all kinds of buildings in which the structure *is* the form and all extra ornament is forbidden. These men were idealistic intellectuals, full of theories about purity and truth in architecture. In their view a good building should be a kind of efficient machine, and what's more, good buildings should inevitably lead to a better society. They invented a radical new aesthetic for a mechanized world. It is called modernism.

Modernism really entered the mainstream in America with the construction of the United Nations Secretariat Building in New York in 1950. It is a sleek and elegant rectangular slab, standing alone like a gigantic sculpture. The two ends are solid marble walls, and the two sides are sheer curtain walls of blue-green glass. It was designed by a committee after a sketch by Le Corbusier, one of the greatest European architects. Unlike anything built before, it pointed the way to a new kind of skyscraper.

In the beginning modernism was almost like a religion, and its prophet in America was a German immigrant, Ludwig Mies van der Rohe. He fled the Nazis in the late 1930s and moved to Chicago, where he taught an entire generation of young architects his principles of order, logic, and clarity. Like Louis Sullivan, Mies had a motto: *Less is more.* This paradox proposes that the simplest things are often the most meaningful. Mies's buildings are stripped down to their essential elements—steel frames and glass curtain walls, marble screens and stone paving. In 1958 a new skyscraper by Mies van der Rohe opened in New York. The Seagram

Previous page:
Manhattan skyline at midcentury

24

The Seagram Buil.

Building is a 38-story tower, modest by New York standards, but monumental in its impact. It is a simple slab, set back from the avenue by a broad plaza with two great fountains. It is utterly spare, but incredibly deluxe, perfectly crafted of the finest materials. The curtain wall is made of amber glass and expensive bronze I-beams, which echo the steel structure underneath. It is the greatest skyscraper of its era, and it was very influential. Everyone began building glass boxes, and as corporate America embraced modernism, not only skyscrapers but buildings of all kinds were built with glass curtain walls and flat tops. They could be practical and efficient and all-purpose, but gradually they began to seem mass-produced. And since most architects are not great artists like Mies, most of these skyscrapers are ordinary and dull.

"Architecture must have something that appeals to the human heart."—Kenzo Tange, architect

At midcentury there was only one great American-born architect with the stature of Mies or Le Corbusier. Frank Lloyd Wright had worked for Louis Sullivan as a very young man, but he took the ideas of form and function in a totally different direction than the Europeans. Instead of the concept of "building as machine," Wright believed in an "organic architecture." He considered a good building to be like a living thing, its form growing in a natural way from its site and materials and purpose. Wright disliked big cities, and he was very ambivalent about skyscrapers. During his entire long career, from the 1890s through the 1950s, he built only a couple of extremely modest towers. But in 1956 he unveiled an astonishing idea for an entire city of 100,000 people living and working in a single megaskyscraper. Wright envisioned an immense spire, *one mile high*, like a spiky crystal surging upward from the prairie, surrounded only by a small town and farms. His proposal included hanging gardens, helicopter pads, and even atomic-powered elevators! Frank Lloyd Wright's mile-high tower was part intellectual exercise and part publicity stunt, but at the same time it offered a spectacular utopian vision for a limitless future.

Down on Earth, during the 1960s and '70s, modernism took many forms. During this era the best and most adventurous architects pushed the boundaries of technology

⊙ THE TWIN TOWERS OF MARINA CITY ⊙

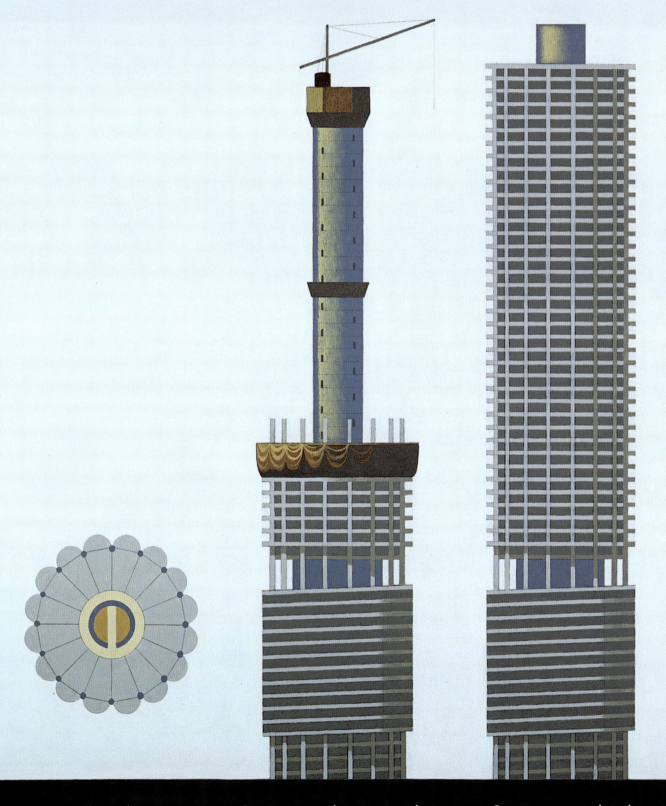

Floor plan   **One tower under construction**   **One tower completed**

to make their buildings stand out among the glass boxes. In Chicago's Marina City complex of 1964, architect Bertram Goldberg built two identical round towers. He did away with the steel frame and instead used reinforced concrete for construction. Concrete poured around steel rods or mesh offers equal strength, and more flexibility of design than the steel frame alone. Reinforced concrete can be formed to make unusual shapes, and the Marina City towers resemble a pair of corncobs. The complex includes apartments, shops, restaurants, banks, and recreation facilities. It was a radical departure in skyscraper design and technology.

Other architects began to treat their buildings as gigantic sculptures. The Transamerica Pyramid, built in San Francisco in the early 1970s, is in the form of an immensely tall, extremely skinny pyramid. When the design was unveiled, it was so controversial that people picketed in the streets wearing dunce caps to mimic the shape of the building. In time it has become a landmark on the skyline.

One of the most beautiful of the "skyscrapers as sculpture" is the John Hancock Tower built in Boston in 1976. From the time the project was announced, it was also controversial. The site was right next to a beloved architectural masterpiece— Trinity Church by H. H. Richardson, one of the greatest American architects of the nineteenth century. Everyone was concerned that an immense office tower would overwhelm the church. Instead, architects I. M. Pei and Henry Cobb made a kind of homage to it. The tower is a beautiful sheer slab, shaped like a prism and sheathed bottom to top in reflective glass.

Perversely, as soon as the tower was completed, the glass panels began popping out and crashing to the street. As they fell, over time, each panel was temporarily replaced with plywood. At one point, the tower was called the "world's tallest wooden building." After it was discovered that the reflective coating interfered with the adhesive used to secure the glass, the problem was solved, and every panel of glass was replaced at immense cost, so that today the entire building acts as a gigantic polished mirror, reflecting the sky and clouds, *and* Trinity Church. The ethereal skyscraper shimmers and changes with the light and the weather. It almost disappears, while the stone church stands firmly grounded and rock-solid beside it.

The John Hancock Tower and Trinity Chu

"Seeing those high risers, bigger and bigger and bigger . . ."

—Louise Nevelson, sculptor

After decades as the unchallenged king of skyscrapers, the Empire State Building suddenly had competition. At the end of the 1960s a new generation of supertall buildings arrived. The first was the 100-story John Hancock Center in Chicago. At 1,127 feet, it was taller than the Chrysler building, but much more massive than the Chrysler's slender tower. The building has the shape of a titanic pylon, with sloping sides. It was also constructed in a new way. Instead of a regular steel frame grid, the outside has enormous cross-braces that zigzag up the building, supporting much of the weight of the structure while absorbing the wind pressure. John Hancock Center is a mixed-use skyscraper. The lower floors are commercial, while the upper floors are luxury apartments. The residents have heart-stopping views. They live so high in the clouds that sometimes they must call the doorman to find out the weather down below on the street. With its dynamic cross-braces, "Big John" is brash and bold. Its design has been called arrogant and swaggering, like "a great cowboy stalking the town."

In the mid-1960s an entire district of lower Manhattan was bulldozed for the construction of two immense skyscrapers. Construction took several years, and when they were finished, the 110-story twin towers of the World Trade Center were the two tallest buildings in the world. The north tower was 1,368 feet tall and the south tower 6 feet shorter. After forty years the Empire State Building was now in third place. The twin towers were constructed with several technical innovations. The exterior walls were a kind of super-lattice of steel, with closely spaced columns supporting much of the weight of the buildings, unlike a regular curtain wall. The elevator system was also something new. Banks of express elevators ascended to several sky lobbies at different levels, where passengers changed to local cars to reach their floors.

The two identical structures stood like colossal cubic pillars in a vast paved plaza. Architectural critics were not enthusiastic. "These are big buildings, but they are not great architecture," wrote the *New York Times*. They were regarded as undistinguished looking, isolated in their bare and uninviting windswept plaza, and simply *too big*. As many as fifty thousand people went to work in the twin towers every day—the entire population of a small city. For many New Yorkers it was almost a sacrilege to build

higher than the Empire State Building, and for a time there was talk of enlarging it to reclaim the crown. Thankfully, this idea was scrapped, and gradually, over time, the twin towers settled into the fabric of the city. In 1974 New Yorkers were surprised and delighted when French aerialist Philippe Petit secured a tightrope between the towers and performed his act a quarter of a mile above the pavement. After a few years, the World Trade Center took its rightful place on the skyline as a beloved landmark—two exclamation points at the tip of Manhattan.

But while they were being completed, an even taller skyscraper was begun in Chicago. Finished in 1974, Sears Tower topped off with 110 floors, and a height of 1,451 feet. For the first time, Chicago was home to the world's tallest building. Sears Tower also has structural innovations. It is built as though nine different buildings, each like a vertical tube, are stacked and bundled together for rigidity and strength. The different tubes end at different heights, so the top has a dramatic profile, a pure rectangular modernist version of a spire. Unfortunately, the site is subject to high winds, and the tower sways enough that windows sometimes break. There is even an urban legend that when his office window shattered, one executive was blown out and back in again!

These behemoths of the early '70s once again raised the old questions about skyscrapers. Immense buildings cause controversy because they do not belong just to their owners. Once they are built, everyone must live with them. They totally transform the neighborhoods in which they are raised. Since they consume enormous amounts of energy and cause congestion, there are very real questions about their worth. Who should make the decisions about building structures that affect everyone? Just how do skyscrapers benefit society? How do skyscrapers contribute or detract from the conditions of life in a city? What form should our cities take? How densely should huge buildings (and people) be packed together? How big is too big?

"Less is a bore." —Robert Venturi, architect

For decades the idea that "less is more" was considered almost a law of architecture, but by the early 1980s strict modernism was beginning to seem like a style of the past, from a period in history that was receding in time. A new spirit was in the air. For the first time in fifty years, decoration and ornament were again

in vogue. Skyscrapers began to be designed once more with elaborate crowns and spires. The new style is called postmodernism.

The most notorious of these new skyscrapers was the AT&T Building, built in New York in 1984. Architect Philip Johnson designed a handsome tower clad in pink granite with a beautiful Renaissance-inspired gold-leafed lobby and grand public loggia. Then, totally unexpectedly, the top of the tower has a gable shape with an enormous round keyhole. The entire building resembles a surreal Chippendale-style highboy. It seemed outrageous and bizarre, almost shocking, but it stood out sharply against the monotonous glass boxes around it, and it was instantly famous. "We were getting bored with the box," Johnson explained.

In his late seventies, Philip Johnson was regarded as the grand old man of American architecture. He was one of modernism's staunchest champions and had actually assisted Mies van der Rohe in designing the Seagram Building. Now he was one of the leaders for change. After the serious ideas of modernism, some of the new generation of skyscrapers were quirky and witty, even humorous. Johnson himself wrote of his new work, "Have fun. Always try to get fun in." As the millennium drew near, the door was wide open for new ideas in the art of skyscraper design.

"Looking upwards knows no limits." —Japanese proverb

Until the 1950s, skyscrapers were built only in America. But during the second half of the twentieth century, as American-style western culture swept the globe, skyscraper technology spread to every part of the world. Some European cities welcomed skyscrapers, but others were more ambivalent. London, for example, has been very slow in accepting tall buildings. Only in the late twentieth century did the skyscraper begin taking hold there. And in Paris tall buildings are banned from the historical center of the city. The Eiffel Tower still stands alone as the city's symbol, while the skyscrapers are clustered together on the outskirts of town. But today most major cities on Earth are dominated by tall buildings, and since the mid-1990s, many of the most interesting skyscraper projects have been built abroad.

Cutting-edge architects continue to experiment with technology, pushing the limits of form and function. One radical skyscraper newly constructed in 1999 is the Burj Al Arab Hotel, built in the oil-rich kingdom of Dubai. (*Burj* is Arabic for "tower.") Here the immense

hotel sits just offshore on its own island. It is a great triangular structure, covered on one side with a taut Teflon membrane. It resembles an enormous billowing sail towering over the flat coastline. There is even a helicopter landing pad high up near the pinnacle. Besides playing with new forms, today architects are making skyscrapers more energy efficient and environmentally friendly. For example, London's novel bullet-shaped skyscraper, the Gherkin, has skycourts that spiral up through the building, providing beautiful parklike public spaces and a natural ventilation system.

Fueled by explosive population growth and expanding economies, the Far East is home to the very latest generation of superskyscrapers. And many of them are pointedly Asian in style. In 1998 a pair of identical skyscrapers, the Petronas Towers, opened in Kuala Lumpur, Malaysia, as part of a vast construction project to modernize the city. They are made of reinforced concrete, clad in gleaming stainless steel, and at 1,483 feet, they were the world's two new tallest buildings. After nearly a quarter century, Sears Tower was now suddenly in third place. With lofty, pointed spires the twin skyscrapers resemble a pair of minarets, towers for calling Muslims to prayer. Architect Cesar Pelli has written, "I tried to respond to the climate, to the dominant Islamic culture, and to the sense of form and patterning that I could perceive in traditional Malaysian building." At the level of the forty-second floor, a narrow skybridge joins the two buildings. The total effect is that of an enormous gateway. Pelli has called it "a portal to the sky . . . a door to the infinite."

Right at the turn of the twenty-first century, Petronas Towers started a new race for the sky. The great cities of the Far East, such as Hong Kong, Singapore, Shanghai, and Taipei, were building great skylines, and the competition for the world's tallest building heated up once more. After only a few years, Petronas Towers was topped by the Taipei Financial Center in 2004, designed as a kind of titanic "technological pagoda" 1,667 feet tall, with traditional Chinese motifs, and sheathed in jade green glass.

Next in line for the prize was the Shanghai World Financial Center, centerpiece of what has been called the "largest building site in the history of the world," the reconstruction of Shanghai's business district. Architect William Pedersen designed the world's "newest tallest" skyscraper in the form of a sheer glass chisel, with a square footprint at the base, and the top tapering to a knife edge. The original plan showed the chisel-blade crown pierced through by an enormous circular opening. This

36

Spires of the Petronas Tow

grand detail was meant to relieve wind pressure and provide a spectacular observation deck. It also referred to Chinese symbolism, in which the earth is represented by a square, and the heavens by a circle. Resembling a traditional oriental moon gate, it offered a link between earth and sky. However, the circular opening also reminded many Chinese of the rising sun symbol of Japan, therefore the very final design of the Shanghai World Financial Center has a trapezoidal opening.

"The time will pass, the building will stand; out of the ashes something new may come." —I. M. Pei, architect

On the crystal clear morning of September 11, 2001, the unthinkable became a bitter reality. In a barbaric act of breathtaking audacity, a band of radical terrorists hijacked commercial airliners and attacked the United States, using the commandeered aircraft as lethal guided missiles. One of these planes plowed directly into the north tower of the World Trade Center in New York. Then, in full view of the TV cameras, yet another plane streaked into the south tower, exploding on contact as the entire nation watched in horror.

At first, the twin towers absorbed the shock of the impacts, but the searing heat of the blazing jet fuel caused the steel frames gradually to buckle, and both towers, once the tallest buildings on Earth, came crashing down in a hail of flying debris, twisted metal, and glass shards. Nearly 3,000 people were murdered.

Six months after the tragedy, a group of artists organized a temporary memorial. At Ground Zero, two mighty beams of light were projected straight up into the night sky over lower Manhattan. These towers of light were visible twenty-five miles away and seemed to reach to infinity. They made a powerful statement—simple, beautiful, and heartbreaking. The symbolic, ghostly "Tribute in Light" literally scraped the sky and emphasized the terrible void in the skyline.

An architectural competition was held to fill that void. The winning entry included space for a moving tribute to the victims of 9/11 in the footprint of the fallen towers. The plan called for a grouping of sharply angled office buildings, resembling gigantic shards of glass, and a magnificent skyscraper that would taper up from a fortified base as its centerpiece. Its crown would be a slender spire slicing skyward to the

The original design of
Shanghai World Financial Ce

lofty height of 1,776 feet in commemoration of July 4, 1776, the date of the American Declaration of Independence. The design of this skyscraper proved to be very controversial. Expectations for the new Freedom Tower were high, and after the experience of 9/11, the design process was highly charged with emotion.

Freedom Tower was planned to be the tallest building on Earth at 1,776 feet, but before it was even begun, another project completely changed the game. The Burj Khalifa in Dubai was finished in 2010, and at an astonishing 2,722 feet, it is over a half mile high—nearly 1,000 feet higher than Freedom Tower, which was not finished until 2014. In the years since the Burj Khalifa was built, a new generation of ultratall skyscrapers have been constructed in Japan, South Korea, Malaysia, Saudi Arabia, and China, which boasts three of these behemoths. As of 2024, Freedom Tower is now merely number nine in the "tallest building" sweepstakes. And even in New York City, once the "capital" of skyscrapers, a new generation of buildings is remaking the familiar skyline. Many of these new structures are "pencil" skyscrapers—extremely tall, extremely skinny buildings built on small plots of land—which are mixed-use structures with floor-through luxury apartments for the superrich, high in the sky.

The drive to build tall has always been part of the human spirit, and with advancing technology, we will be able to build higher and higher. And being human, if we can we will. Now, for better or for worse, the skyscraper has taken its place as the dominant architecture of the modern world. From the utterly practical idea of a machine that makes the land pay, to the poetic and romantic notions of a lofty gateway to the heavens or a soaring tower of freedom, for more than a century the skyscraper has been one of the most potent symbols of success and of our hopes for a brilliant future. Perhaps by the beginning of the next century Frank Lloyd Wright's utopian vision will become reality, and people will live and work in vast vertical cities with all the necessities of life available under one roof, megaskyscrapers thousands of feet tall—amazing technological wonders, and the most complex and massive structures ever made. Only the sky is the limit.

"To build well is an act of peace." —Kevin Roche, architect

SEARS
TOWER

1,451 ft.   Chicago, 1974

PETRONAS
TOWERS

1,483 ft.   Kuala Lumpur, Malaysia, 1998

TAIPEI
FINANCIAL CENTER

1,667 ft.   Taipei, 2004

SHANGHAI WORLD
FINANCIAL CENTER

1,614 ft.   Shanghai, 2008

FREEDOM
TOWER

1,776 ft.   New York, 2014

THE BURJ

2,716 ft.   Dubai, 2009

FRANK LLOYD WRIGHT'S
MILE HIGH TOWER CONCEPT

PARADE OF SKYSCRAPERS
DRAWN TO SCALE

When constructed, each of these buildings was (or will be) the tallest skyscraper in the world.*

SINGER BUILDING
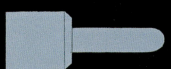
600 ft.   New York, 1908

METROPOLITAN LIFE TOWER
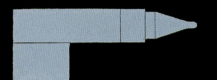
700 ft.   New York, 1909

WOOLWORTH BUILDING

800 ft.   New York, 1913

CHRYSLER BUILDING
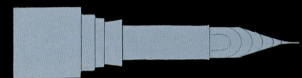
1,046 ft.   New York, 1930

EMPIRE STATE BUILDING

1,250 ft.   New York, 1931

WORLD TRADE CENTER

North Tower 1,368 ft.   New York, 1973
South Tower 1,362 ft.   New York, 1973

*(note: antennae added after the building was built do not count in the height record, and thus are not shown)

BIBLIOGRAPHY

Able, Chris. *Skyhigh: Vertical Architecture*. London: Royal Academy of Arts, 2003.

Dupré, Judith. *Skyscrapers: A History of the World's Most Famous and Important Skyscrapers*. New York: Black Dog & Leventhal, 1996.

Ferriss, Hugh. *The Metropolis of Tomorrow*. New York: Ives Washburn, Publisher, 1929. Facsimile edition, New York: Princeton Architectural Press, 1986.

Goldberger, Paul. *The Skyscraper*. New York: Alfred A. Knopf, 1982.

Howeler, Eric. *Skyscraper*. New York: Universal Publishing, 2003.

Huxtable, Ada Louise. *The Tall Building Artistically Reconsidered: The Search for a Skyscraper Style*. New York: Pantheon, 1984.

Sabbagh, Karl. *Skyscraper: The Making of a Building*. New York: Viking, 1990.

Stravitz, David. *The Chrysler Building: Creating a New York Icon, Day by Day*. New York: Princeton Architectural Press, 2002.

Terranova, Antonio. *Skyscrapers*. Vercelli, Italy: White Star, 2003.

Wagner, Geraldine. *Thirteen Months to Go: The Creation of the Empire State Building*. San Diego: Thunder Bay Press, 2003.

Because the process of designing and building skyscrapers is so complex, plans and projections often change during construction, and the details of their design and even their height are constantly evolving.

: CAPTIONS :

Cover: The Chrysler and Empire State Buildings, day and night
Half title page: Architects in costume as their buildings at the Beaux Arts Ball of 1931
Title page: The spire of the Empire State Building was planned as a dock for airships

ATHENEUM BOOKS FOR YOUNG READERS
An imprint of Simon & Schuster Children's Publishing Division
1230 Avenue of the Americas, New York, New York 10020
© 2007 by Lynn Curlee
Book design by Krista Vossen
All rights reserved, including the right of reproduction in whole or in part in any form.
ATHENEUM BOOKS FOR YOUNG READERS is a registered trademark of Simon & Schuster, LLC.
Atheneum logo is a trademark of Simon & Schuster, LLC.
For information about special discounts for bulk purchases, please contact Simon & Schuster
Special Sales at 1-866-506-1949 or business@simonandschuster.com.
The Simon & Schuster Speakers Bureau can bring authors to your live event. For more
information or to book an event, contact the Simon & Schuster Speakers Bureau at
1-866-248-3049 or visit our website at www.simonspeakers.com.
The text for this book was set in Meta.
The illustrations for this book were rendered in acrylic on canvas.
Mr. Curlee would like to thank Ed Peterson for photographing the paintings.
Manufactured in China
0225 SCP
This Atheneum Books for Young Readers edition July 2025
2 4 6 8 10 9 7 5 3 1
Library of Congress Cataloging-in-Publication Data
Names: Curlee, Lynn, 1947- author.
Title: Skyscraper / Lynn Curlee.
Description: Atheneum edition. | New York : Atheneum Books for Young Readers, [2025] |
Includes bibliographical references. | Audience: Ages 7 up | Summary: "From the Empire State
Building to the Chrysler Building, to the Sears and Hancock Towers, to the Petronas Towers in
Kuala Lumpur, to the former World Trade Center, Curlee captures all the drama, excitement, and
tragedy of humanity's attempt to reach ever closer to the clouds"—Provided by publisher.
Identifiers: LCCN 2024029817 | ISBN 9781665969079 (hardcover) | ISBN
9781665969062 (paperback) | ISBN 9781665969086 (ebook)
Subjects: LCSH: Skyscrapers—History—Juvenile literature. | CYAC: Skyscrapers—History.
Classification: LCC NA6230 .C87 2025 | DDC 720/.483—dc23/eng/20240816
LC record available at https://lccn.loc.gov/2024029817